FACTS AMERICA

BIRDS

PHILIP PERRY AND ELLEN WEISS

SMITHMARK

About the authors

A lifelong naturalist, Philip Perry has traveled the globe in search of wildlife. Interested in all aspects of the natural world, he has authored books on birds, gorillas, reptiles, and trees. His knowledge and understanding of animal behavior have proved to be valuable assets when carrying out his principal passion—wildlife photography.

Ellen Weiss, a children's writer since 1972, has published more than 50 books and many science articles, and has also written television shows and videos for children. Ms. Weiss has received the Children's Choice Award three times. Her latest novel, *The Poof Point*, was written with her husband, Mel Friedman. She lives with him and their daughter, Nora, in New York City.

Editor:
Philip de Ste. Croix

Designer:
Stonecastle Graphics Ltd

Picture research:
Leora Kahn

Coordinating editors:
Andrew Preston
Kristen Schilo

Production:
Ruth Arthur
Sally Connolly
Neil Randles
Andrew Whitelaw

Production editor:
Didi Charney

Director of production:
Gerald Hughes

Typesetter:
Pagesetters Incorporated

Color and monochrome reproduction:
Advance Laser Graphic Arts, Hong Kong

Printed and bound in Hong Kong by
Leefung-Asco Printers Ltd

1992 Colour Library Books Ltd
Godalming Business Centre
Woolsack Way, Godalming
Surrey GU7 1XW, United Kingdom
CLB 2608

This edition published in 1992 by
SMITHMARK Publishers Inc.
112 Madison Avenue
New York, NY 10016 USA

SMITHMARK books are available for bulk purchase for sales promotion and premium use. For details, write or call the manager of special sales, SMITHMARK Publishers Inc., 112 Madison Avenue, New York, NY 10016; (212) 532-6600.

Library of Congress Cataloging-in-Publication Data

Perry, Philip, 1956–
    Facts America. Birds / Philip Perry & Ellen Weiss.
       p.   cm.
    Includes bibliographical references and index.
    Summary: Introduces a variety of the birds that are to be found in the cities, woodlands, mountains, and other parts of North America.
    ISBN 0-8317-2315-7 (hardcover)
    1. Birds—Juvenile literature. [1. Birds.] I. Weiss, Ellen, 1949–   II. Title. III. Title: Birds.
    QL676.2.P45   1992
    598.297—dc20   92-9403

These spectacular birds are greater flamingos. Their long legs and necks and beautifully colored plumage are unmistakable. In the United States, these birds are likely to be seen only on the Florida mud flats, where they use their bills to strain small marine animals from the mud.

Contents

1

THE AMAZING TUBE NOSES: Birds that spend their whole lives wandering the world's oceans, only landing to breed, are called pelagic. Albatrosses, shearwaters, and petrels are common pelagic birds. Bird-watchers call them tube noses, because they have long, tubelike external nostrils.

Masters of their environment, albatrosses cross the oceans on narrow wings that are as much as ten feet across. These birds are so perfectly designed for gliding that they hardly ever need to flap their wings.

Albatrosses perform elaborate mating dances at their nesting colonies, snapping their bills and bowing their heads. These strangely hypnotic rituals serve to forge such strong bonds between breeding pairs that many albatrosses remain with their chosen partners until death.

TINY VOYAGERS: It hardly seems possible that storm petrels can survive the hardships of their ocean habitat. Yet these tiny seabirds, which are smaller than robins, are quite at home even in raging winds and towering seas. In calmer waters, they patter across the surface on webbed feet, held up by rapidly fluttering wings. This unique habit has given rise to the name *petrel*, which refers to the biblical story of Saint Peter walking on water.

CUTTING THE WATER: Shearwaters mostly eat squid and fish plucked from the surface or caught after a shallow dive.

These surface-skimming dives are the reason for this bird's name. Shearwaters like to live in groups, and migrating flocks can number in the millions. To protect their eggs from predators, many shearwaters nest in underground burrows that they only visit at night.

▲ *Wedge-tailed shearwaters make their nests in Pacific waters.*

◀ *These black-footed albatrosses, or gooney birds, attract one another by dancing. Their colony is on the Pacific island of Midway, where there is a U.S. naval base. Now that naval activity on the island has lessened, the birds are being allowed to flourish.*

Effortlessly gliding on ▶ an updraft, a northern fulmar sails over its sea-cliff home. Light-colored birds like this one are most common in Atlantic waters.

▲ *Watched by a neighbor, two Laysan albatrosses engage in a stately courting ceremony.*

◀ *A greater shearwater takes a rest from diving after squid. To become airborne again, it must patter across the surface on its large webbed feet until it builds up enough momentum for lift-off. Each fall, some 200,000 greater shearwaters flock together off Cape Cod, Massachusetts.*

Cliff Nesters

▼ Cormorants use seaweed, sticks, and grasses, as well as our seaborne litter, to build their nests. Nylon ropes and fishing lines are often used as building materials, sometimes with fatal results, when hopelessly entangled birds are accidentally hanged.

The two puffins in the ▶ middle are "billing," a common courtship behavior in which paired birds crouch low and noisily slap each other's bills from side to side. Bouts of billing may end with a more gentle nuzzling of bills.

▲ Each of these Brandt's cormorants has nested just outside its neighbors' reach.

They are aggressive birds, and nestlings must not stray from the safety of the nest.

CLIFF-HANGERS: There are 22 different kinds of auks, and 20 of them are found along the coasts of North America. They are pelagic, normally only landing to breed, and they like to make their nesting places on high cliffs. The auk family includes puffins, murres, and dovekies.

EGG ROLL: The densely packed seabird cities of auks can create special problems. Sometimes when neighboring adults land, eggs can break accidentally. One kind of auk, the common murre, has solved the problem in a unique way: It lays sharply pointed eggs that roll in a tight circle instead of falling off the narrow rock ledges.

PENGUIN COUSINS: Auks have a lot in common with their cousins in the Southern Hemisphere, the penguins. Auks and penguins both use stubby wings to swim to great depths underwater, chasing fish or crustaceans. Unlike penguins, all auks can fly. The only exception was the great auk, which sadly became extinct in 1852.

USING THE CORMORANT: The cormorant, which is not an auk, is another cliff dweller. Cormorants have long been exploited by people. Their droppings, found in great quantities at their crowded nesting sites, are used for fertilizer. In China, fishermen sometimes use the birds to catch fish. A line is tied around the cormorant's neck, and when the bird catches a fish, the line prevents the cormorant from eating it. The fisherman then pulls the bird in and takes the fish.

▲ *This tufted puffin, which lives on the Pacific coast, is wearing its beautiful summer breeding colors. In winter, it will have drab plumage (feathers), no tufts, and dull bill colors—quite a contrast.*

◄ *Nesting close together helps common murres protect one another against attack. The nearness of each bird's neighbors makes it much harder for predatory gulls to find the murres' chicks or eggs.*

Fishers and Pirates

LIVING ARROWHEADS: Seabirds use many fishing techniques to reap the ocean's bounty of fish. Northern gannets, which live along the Atlantic coastline, are the most spectacular fishers. Diving from great heights, gannets sweep back their wings to transform themselves into living arrowheads an instant before breaking the surface of the water.

Skimmers, also East Coast birds, are amazingly adapted for catching fish. They have huge lower bills, which they "plow" through the water as they fly low with open mouths. This lets them scoop up any small fish swimming near the surface.

SKY PIRATES: Jaegers breed in Alaska and northern Canada, but winter in South America. Although they eat fish, these birds often prefer not to catch their own. Instead, they patrol the outskirts of colonies of terns, another kind of seabird. The jaegers look for birds carrying food to their mates and nestlings. Then they chase the terns and force them to drop their catch.

Frigate birds are beautifully adapted for fast, evasive flight, but because their feathers easily become waterlogged, they never land on the ocean. If they did, it would be a struggle to take off again. Unable to dive after prey, frigate birds rely heavily on piracy for their food. At their breeding colonies in the Florida Keys, frigate birds harass brown pelicans, terns, and gulls for food. However, frigate birds are actually quite capable of getting

their own food. For instance, they can snatch up dead fish or floating jellyfish from the surface.

ANYTHING FOR A BITE: Most gulls are notorious scavengers and eat almost anything. They follow boats to collect the garbage thrown into the water. Heermann's gulls often forage for shrimps and shellfish along the shoreline, but they will also chase pelicans or boobies and force them to give up their catch.

◀ Heermann's gulls are unusual in their breeding and migrating habits. They breed on the west coast of Mexico and migrate north along the Pacific coast in winter.

This sandwich tern has to hold on very tightly to the wriggling eel in its beak. Otherwise, it risks losing its prize to a thieving frigate bird or gull, even though the tern is a swift flier. This meal must get to the hungry chicks waiting at the tern's nesting site.

This male magnificent frigate ▶ bird has fully inflated his scarlet throat pouch. He is trying to attract a female flying overhead and entice her down to the nest site he has chosen. He will also vibrate his wings and cry a haunting, trembling call.

▼ These northern gannets will hunt for herring and mackerel to feed to their chicks. Gannets' skulls are reinforced to cushion their impact with the sea as the birds dive from great heights for fish.

Even when they are not scooping up fish with their extraordinary bills, black skimmers are easy to spot because of their unusual facial coloring.

Staying Alive

ADAPTING TO SURVIVE: Many birds have developed interesting adaptations to help their species survive. Ducks are a good example. In most duck species, the males are easy to tell apart from the females. There are usually obvious differences in size, plumage (another word for feathers), and other features. Male harlequin ducks, for example, have striking, multicolored plumage. Female harlequins are much more drab, with dark brown bodies and pale breasts. There is a reason for their dull coloring: Since only the females usually sit on the eggs, they must be well camouflaged to avoid attracting the attention of predators. On the other hand, the males, or drakes, are gaily colored in order to attract mates. But as soon as nesting has begun, and the drakes no longer need to impress possible mates, they molt, or shed their old feathers to reveal new ones. Their new color is dull, like the females'.

SAFETY IN NUMBERS: Old-squaws, also called longtail ducks, often build their nests in the middle of colonies of Arctic terns. Odd as this may seem, there is good reason for it. Arctic terns are notoriously aggressive birds when breeding, constantly alert to any threat of danger. Dozens of terns immediately skirmish with any jaeger, fox, or human being bold enough to approach their eggs or chicks. All this defensive action is obviously helpful to the old-squaws that are nesting inside the terns' territory.

SALT? NO PROBLEM: Brant look like small, dark Canada geese. They have some special equipment, though. Brant have salt glands, which remove salts from the bloodstream. This means that they can exist on a winter diet of eelgrass, sea lettuce, and other saltwater plants, without getting sick and dehydrated. These glands are so efficient that brant can actually drink seawater.

Pelicans are known to live more than 20 years. Many of them return to the same nesting sites year after year, finding the same mates every year.

▲ This old-squaw is wearing its winter plumage. It has lost the long tail it had in the summer. Male old-squaws are the only ducks that have three different plumages during the year.

▼ In the summer months, harlequin ducks, like this male, live along fast-flowing rivers. Harlequins dive very well, swimming their way upstream to sift the riverbed for food.

◄ Brant nest farther north than any other species of goose. Their breeding grounds extend to the high arctic seacoasts of Alaska, Greenland, and Canada. To prevent their eggs from getting cold, female brant pluck large numbers of down feathers from their own breasts for nest linings. Male brant do not sit on the eggs but do stand guard near the nests to fend off predators and to raise the goslings.

▼ Because their legs are positioned at the very backs of their bodies, common loons have difficulty walking on land. Not surprisingly, loons build their nests, like this one, as close as possible to the water. Loons are extremely sensitive to disturbance when nesting, so the presence of breeding loons is a good indicator of a true wilderness area.

Shoreline Birds

BETWEEN SEA AND LAND: The margin between sea and land plays host to all kinds of birdlife. There are both full-time residents and visitors that pause only for nourishment before continuing their passage.

JUST OPEN AND SERVE: Oystercatchers live along both coasts, where their shrill, piping call is a familiar sound. Equipped with sturdy, bright red bills, oystercatchers pry apart oysters and mussels, and make short work of hammering open crab shells. They nest above the high-tide mark in shallow depressions formed in the ground. Oystercatchers lay two or three eggs, which are very difficult to spot among shells and pebbles on the beach.

TOY BIRDS: Sanderlings look like mechanical toys as they run along the water's edge in a frantic effort to snap up small shrimp and other crustaceans exposed by the waves' backwash. Among the world's greatest migrants, some sanderlings make a twice-yearly journey between southernmost Chile and their high arctic breeding grounds.

Seaside sparrows live in salt marshes and mangroves. Oversize feet help prevent them from sinking into the fine mud as they scamper around in search of seeds and insects.

VISITORS: Horned larks, on the other hand, are only casual winter visitors to coasts. They like sand dunes, where they often form mixed flocks with other birds such as snow buntings and Lapland longspurs. Their horns, actually short feather tufts, are hard to see from a distance.

▲ *In winter, sanderlings have a lot of white in their plumage. Come spring, they are transformed, turning a brilliant rust red. Sometimes two clutches, or groups, of eggs are laid at once. One is sat on by the male, and the other, by his mate. Each bird raises his or her own chicks.*

Surfbirds are common ▶ on rocky beaches along the Pacific coast during winter. In the summer, they nest atop Alaska's mountains.

American oystercatchers look after their young with greater parental care than most other shorebirds do. The young birds need enough time to learn from their parents how oystercatchers are supposed to catch and eat their food, which consists of crabs, clams, and other mollusks. It can take up to a year for the young to master all the various feeding techniques.

▼ This ruddy turnstone is probing wet sand for crabs. The bird gets its name from the strategy it uses to find morsels of food on stony beaches. The turnstone finds hidden worms, sand fleas, and other insects by flipping over stones and seaweed with its beak.

▼ In many bird species, the males display, or show off, for females that are potential mates. Horned larks often deliver their songs in display flights. Having risen high in the air, the males sing while flying in circles, before dropping back to earth.

2

A LARGE FAMILY: The heron family, found almost all over the United States, includes egrets and bitterns in addition to herons. Preferring waterside habitats, these birds all have long necks, long legs, and daggerlike bills. America's largest heron, the great blue heron, has the most wide-ranging territory. Usually observed standing at the edges of lakes or swamps, great blue herons wait patiently for fish to swim within striking distance.

During the breeding season, great egrets develop splendid, flowing white plumes that cascade down their backs. Egrets, especially snowy egrets, were once slaughtered all over the world for their plumes, which were used in women's hats.

THE TALENTED GREENBACK: A harsh *kyow* call is often the first clue to the presence of the green-backed heron as it takes flight, trailing its yellow legs beyond its tail. In Japan, green-backed herons have developed an astonishing fishing technique. They deliberately place an insect or twig on the water and crouch and wait for fish to be lured by the bait. Because of this extraordinary behavior, green-backed herons are among those very few animals worldwide that are known to have learned how to use a tool.

SHY BIRDS: Bitterns and night herons are very shy in nature. It is not easy to spot them. By day, they hide in dense bushes or reedbeds and only come to life when dusk falls. If a bittern is startled in the open, it instantly freezes, bill pointing toward the sky, relying on its streaked plumage to camouflage it against a background of marsh grasses.

◀ *While night herons sometimes do hunt during the day, they often are harassed by larger, daytime herons. They prefer hunting under the protective cloak of darkness. This black-crowned night heron's large crimson eyes are designed for excellent night vision.*

▲ *Although this young least bittern still has not lost all its down feathers, it reacts to danger just the way an adult does—by freezing stock-still, head skyward. Unfortunately, this alarm posture will not disguise the little bird very well against its green background.*

Worldwide, 30 types of green-backed heron have been described. Three of them are found in the United States. They spend their winters in Florida and southern California. Like most herons, greenbacks like marshy areas with dense vegetation.

▼ Like many birds that build large nesting platforms, great blue herons prefer places they have chosen in previous years. That way, they use up less energy gathering fresh materials for the nests. Over time, old nests become very bulky, providing safer homes for nestlings.

◄ Great egrets are able to eat highly venomous snakes such as water moccasins and cottonmouths, as well as fish, frogs, and salamanders.

Wading Birds

WADERS: Wading birds are those birds that usually wade, instead of swimming or diving, when looking for food. This grouping is fairly arbitrary and covers birds as different from one another as flamingos, spoonbills, and avocets. In spite of their differences, though, wading birds share several common features that reflect their similar life-styles, such as long necks, legs, and bills.

AVOCETS AND STILTS: The title "most graceful American wading bird" might fall to one of two contenders: American avocets or black-necked stilts. Avocets' bodies are beautifully contrasted by cinnamon heads and necks. As these birds wade in shallow water, they swish their delicately upturned bills from side to side to pick up shrimps and insect larvae. Black-necked stilts have even daintier, finer-pointed bills and long pink legs. Avocets and stilts often group together.

▲ *This common snipe is using its long, straight bill to probe the bottom mud of a pool. Sensitive to touch, its bill snaps shut on any insects it brushes against. Spines on the snipe's tongue help carry food to its mouth.*

▲ *When nesting in hot climates, black-necked stilts soak their breast feathers with water to keep themselves and their eggs or nestlings cool. To combat the shimmering heat of a sunburned nest site, they may need to make as many as 100 trips per day to a nearby lake or marsh.*

THE FISHPOND PROBLEM: Wood storks have acutely sensitive beaks that snap shut by reflex the instant they touch a fish or frog. This is why these birds can hunt in even the murkiest pools. Sometimes they even stir up mud to disturb any fish hiding on the bottom. In Florida, ponds made by alligators are an important source of food for wood storks. The birds know by instinct that at certain times of year, the water levels in the ponds will drop. This means that the ponds become very dense with fish. Without these dependable supplies of fish, wood storks have a hard time finding enough food for their hungry nestlings. Because of this, wood storks often do not have babies when there is unusual flooding in dry season or if the ponds dry out completely.

◀ *Although their plumage is identical, male and female American avocets can be told apart by their bills. The very distinctive upturn to this avocet's bill proves that it is a female. Males have straighter, slightly shorter bills. However, in overall size, males are somewhat larger than females.*

▼ *Seen close up, this glossy ibis is full of subtle color, but from afar, it looks entirely black. Glossy ibis are very fond of crayfish. The birds' long, curved bills are ideally suited for pulling these crustaceans from their holes.*

▲ *Wood storks are on America's endangered species list. There are two main reasons for this: the destruction of their habitat following the logging of swamp cypress trees, and human tampering with the environment in Florida's Everglades. Wood storks are especially sensitive to changes in water levels; when levels are low and the food supply dwindles, wood stork colonies often fail to rear any young at all.*

Waterfowl and Water Birds

WATERFOWL: As a group, ducks, geese, and swans are known as waterfowl. Waterfowl have long been associated with humans and were among the very first birds to be domesticated. For centuries, waterfowl in the wild have been targets for hunters, and many have also been raised as food.

During courtship displays, trumpeter swans more than live up to their name. The largest of the world's swans, trumpeters issue their distinctive calls as mated pairs loudly proclaim ownership of their domains.

Male wood ducks are unmistakable because of their unusually patterned heads and

▲ *The metallic blue flash on the male mallard's wings usually cannot be seen when the bird is at rest. This flash is a feature common to many ducks. During courtship, the male bird shows it off to a female as he preens behind his wing. Other courtship displays include head shaking, pursuit flights, tail wagging, and bill dipping.*

◀ *In the 1930s, trumpeter swans were practically extinct in North America, killed for their skins, feathers, and meat. Though they are still rare, their population is once again increasing because they are now protected by law.*

▲ *This American coot chick is called precocial, a term that applies to young birds that can readily move around on their own soon after hatching. Their eyes are open when they hatch, and they are covered with down feathers.*

During the breeding ▶ *season, the pied-billed grebe has the black throat and white black-banded bill you see here. In winter, its bill is dull yellow and its chin is whitish.*

crests. Their favorite feeding technique is called dabbling: They upend themselves in shallow water to get seeds and plants from the bottom.

THE GROUCHY COOT: There are many other birds that are ordinarily found near fresh water, such as grebes and coots, and they go by the more general name of water birds. American coots are fiercely territorial all year and often have fights with other coots. Sitting back in the water, two coots battle to grab each other's toes while stabbing with their bills. They also try to hold their opponents underwater. As usual in the animal world, such disputes rarely cause any serious damage. The weaker bird merely scuttles away in defeat.

FEATHER EATERS: Pied-billed grebes have what seems to be a peculiar craving for eating feathers. The explanation for this strange behavior is that by swallowing a lot of feathers, grebes probably are protecting their stomach linings from injury by fish bones, which they cannot crush before eating.

▼ *Wood ducks live by wooded lakes, eat tree seeds, and make their nests in tree hollows. When they hatch, wood ducklings launch* | *themselves from the nest entrance. Their sheer lightness helps them float gently to the ground and land unharmed.*

Fishers

OUR NOBLE BIRD: Swamps, lakes, rivers, and other inland waters are rich fishing grounds that attract all kinds of birds. Among the noblest of these are bald eagles. Unfortunately, the number of bald eagles has declined all across America. Our national bird is now on the endangered list in many states. Illegal shooting, loss of waterside habitats, and pesticide poisoning have all contributed to the bald eagle's desperate plight. As the public has become more aware of the problem in recent years, many conservation projects have been established to try to reverse the situation. While some progress has been made, it is only in Alaska that large numbers of bald eagles still thrive. There, up to 4,000 of the birds gather every fall along the Chilkat River to gorge themselves on the feast offered by thousands of dying salmon, exhausted after their once-in-a-lifetime journey up the river to spawn.

MAGNIFICENT HUNTERS: Nothing can match the splendor of an osprey hunting. After spotting a large trout near the surface, this amazing fisher flies low over the water, dropping onto its prey like a stone, talons extended. Then, beating its powerful wings hard, the osprey finally manages to get airborne. Tiny spines cover ospreys' feet to help them keep a grip on their wriggling, slippery prey. Often, bald eagles take advantage of the superior fishing skills of ospreys, chasing the more lightly built ospreys and forcing them to drop their hard-earned catch.

POUCH FISHING: American white pelicans are huge birds that can be found in the western part of the continent. Their enormous bill-pouches can take in about three gallons of water. The water is squeezed out at the corners of the mouth, leaving behind a pouchful of fish. White pelicans, which do not dive, often fish cooperatively. They gather in tight flocks to chase shoals of fish into the shallows where they can be scooped up.

▲ *When it has caught a fish, an osprey flies to a favorite feeding perch. After resting for a while to make sure the fish is dead, the bird will begin to eat. Holding the prey firmly in its feet, the osprey tears it into small pieces with its hooked bill, usually starting with the head and leaving the guts.*

This bird is called a common merganser. It is part of an odd group of birds named sawbills, which really do have sawlike teeth on their bills. These teeth help the sawbills hang on to slippery fish.

Like many fish-eating ▶ hunters, bald eagles are very vocal. They call to announce their claim to a territory or to keep contact with a mate. When courting, bald eagle pairs do marvelous aerial gymnastics, somersaulting over and over together with their talons locked.

▼ American white pelicans instinctively increase the chances of their young's survival by hatching their eggs all at the same time. This shortens the amount of time that helpless nestlings can be found in the colony. Predators enjoy a glut of pelican chicks, but only for a very short time. In this way, far more of the offspring survive.

▲ This belted kingfisher has caught a perch. It will kill the fish by repeatedly beating it on a branch. The fish will then be flung in the air and swallowed headfirst, so that its scales do not stick in the bird's throat.

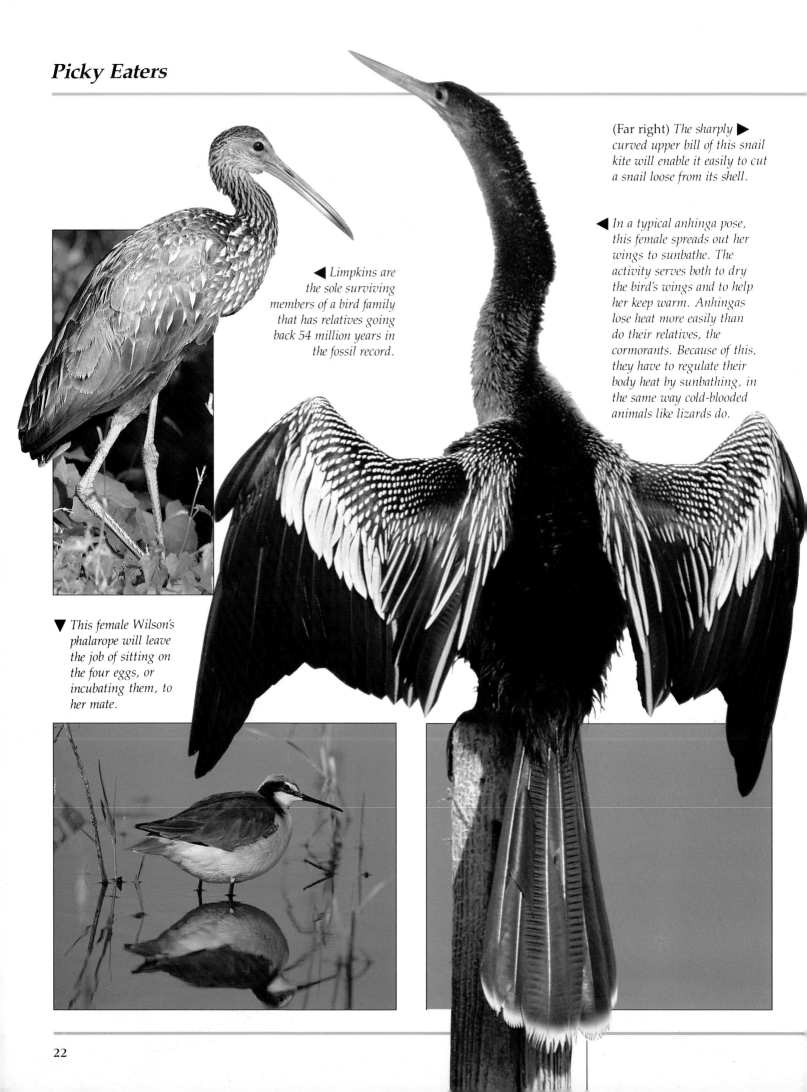

Picky Eaters

◄ Limpkins are the sole surviving members of a bird family that has relatives going back 54 million years in the fossil record.

(Far right) The sharply ► curved upper bill of this snail kite will enable it easily to cut a snail loose from its shell.

◄ In a typical anhinga pose, this female spreads out her wings to sunbathe. The activity serves both to dry the bird's wings and to help her keep warm. Anhingas lose heat more easily than do their relatives, the cormorants. Because of this, they have to regulate their body heat by sunbathing, in the same way cold-blooded animals like lizards do.

▼ This female Wilson's phalarope will leave the job of sitting on the four eggs, or incubating them, to her mate.

YUM! SNAILS! Snail kites and limpkins, both Florida birds, are two kinds of birds that love snails. In fact, snail kites can exist on a diet of nothing but apple snails. Because of this extreme specialization, snail kites (once called Everglade kites) only live in marshy regions where apple snails are abundant. A kite will swoop down and snatch up a snail floating at the surface. Then it will fly to a favorite feeding perch, hold the snail in one foot, and deftly cut the muscle that holds the snail's body to its shell. Snail kites are endangered in the United States because the swamps where they find their food have been drained. However, these birds are still common in countries to the south.

HELPFUL BILLS: Limpkins have specially adapted bills that help them eat their favorite foods. The bills curve to the right at their tips. This makes it easier for the birds to remove snails and mussels from their shells.

Spoonbills, which are closely related to ibis, have very distinctive bills that are broadened and rounded at the end. When fishing, a spoonbill holds its bill slightly open and sweeps it from side to side. As soon as the nerves inside the bill sense contact with a frog or other likely edible object, the bill-snapping reflex is triggered and the bird seizes the prey.

The anhinga is able to swim so low in the water that only its head and neck show, which explains its other name: the snakebird. Anhingas have sharply pointed, daggerlike bills to spear fish and young alligators. The speared prey are tossed into the air and then caught and swallowed headfirst in one neat movement.

TWIRLERS: Phalaropes occasionally use a very strange feeding strategy. Spinning around and around on the water, they daintily pick mosquito larvae and other tiny foods from the surface. It is thought that the twirling action brings food up from the bottom.

◀ *Early this century, when the plume trade was at its height, the roseate spoonbill's splendid pink feathers nearly caused its downfall. After a long fight, preservationists (the forerunners of today's conservationists) at last ended the fashion for feathers.*

City Parks and Suburban Lawns

A HOME IN YOUR BACKYARD: If you want to attract birds into your backyard, a good way to do it, in addition to providing food and water, is to furnish them with birdhouses. About 50 species of American birds will use these specially built nesting boxes. Putting the boxes up is a good way of helping your local birds. It can be especially valuable in places where natural nest holes are scarce because trees have been cut down.

DIFFERENT HOMES FOR DIFFERENT BIRDS: You can make or buy birdhouses in a variety of designs, each built with a particular type of bird in mind. The dimensions of the house, especially the entrance, are crucial in determining which species of bird will nest there. For instance, house wrens will occupy a birdhouse with a one-inch diameter entrance hole, but eastern bluebirds need an entrance at least one and a half inches across. Woodpeckers often enlarge small entrance holes so they can get into birdhouses designed for chickadees.

Instead of enclosed boxes, some birds prefer houses with shelves, a roof, and one or more sides left open. Open platforms more closely resemble the nest sites chosen by these birds. If you want to tempt barn swallows or robins, try placing nesting shelves in the eaves of your roof.

Purple martins are very social birds, and their houses are generally built in one or more sections, each containing eight separate apartments. Unusually big martin houses have contained an astonishing 270 pairs of birds.

DO NOT DISTURB: Eastern screech owls need quite large birdhouses, which should be placed far enough away from your house so that the owls' loud and repetitive calls do not disturb you at night.

It is important to approach an owl's home very carefully. Although screech owls are less sensitive than other types of owls, all owls are very touchy about being disturbed. They have acute hearing, can fly soundlessly, and will not hesitate to strike anyone coming too close.

▲ *Prothonotary warblers have an unusual nesting habit. First, the males establish several nests in territories they claim when they arrive at their summer quarters. Then, ignoring the "dummy" nests, the females build the nests that are actually used to raise their young.*

This apartment house, ▶ *intended for purple martins, is shared by house sparrows. They often compete with the martins for nesting places. Male martins get their partners by moving into a room in a birdhouse and defending it. Then each female chooses a room—and with it a mate.*

Birdhouse Visitors

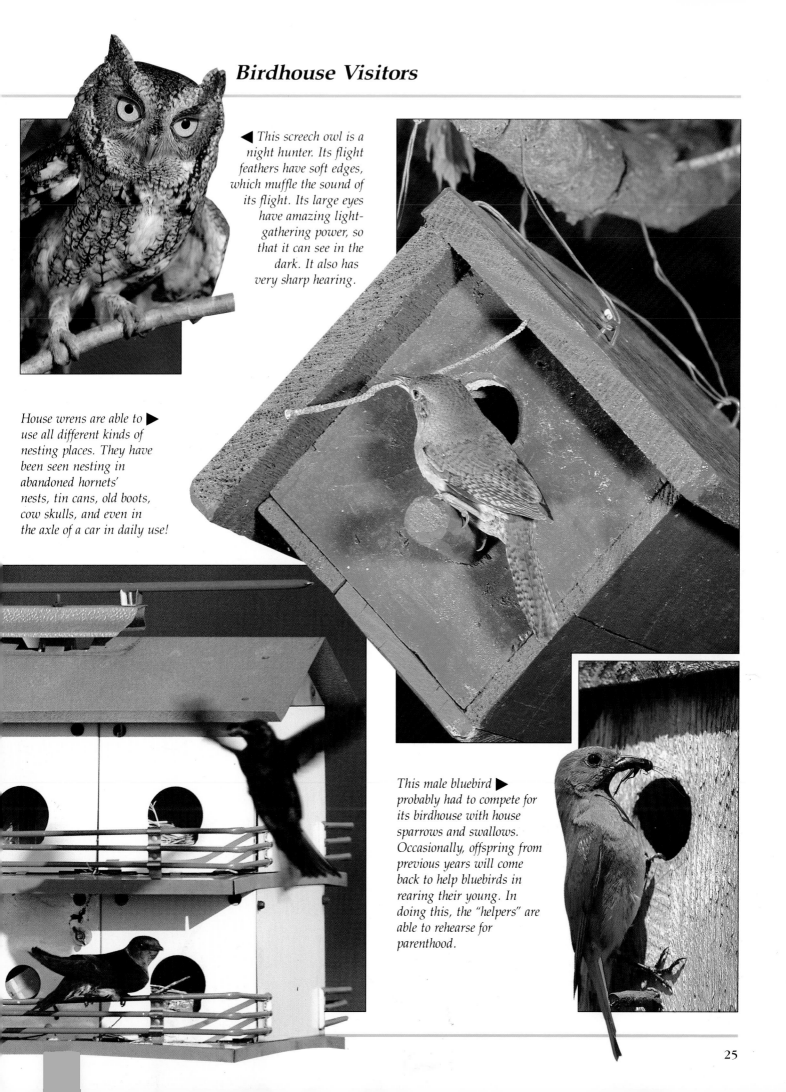

◀ This screech owl is a night hunter. Its flight feathers have soft edges, which muffle the sound of its flight. Its large eyes have amazing light-gathering power, so that it can see in the dark. It also has very sharp hearing.

House wrens are able to ▶ use all different kinds of nesting places. They have been seen nesting in abandoned hornets' nests, tin cans, old boots, cow skulls, and even in the axle of a car in daily use!

This male bluebird ▶ probably had to compete for its birdhouse with house sparrows and swallows. Occasionally, offspring from previous years will come back to help bluebirds in rearing their young. In doing this, the "helpers" are able to rehearse for parenthood.

Park and Lawn Lovers

THE EARLY BIRD: A variety of birds, from robins to doves, like to live in parks, lawns, and other neatly trimmed areas of grass. Robins find lawns and golf courses ideal hunting grounds for earthworms. Cocking their heads to one side, robins keep an eye out for worms emerging from their burrows, pouncing quick as a flash on any that do.

Most woodpeckers rarely venture down to the ground, but northern flickers are an exception. They forage on lawns for ants, their main food source.

As dusk falls, common nighthawks leave their daytime hiding places to hunt over open parklands. Nighthawks have tiny bills but phenomenally wide, gaping mouths that are very efficient at catching flying insects. Some nighthawks have abandoned their traditional open-pasture nesting grounds and instead have taken up residence on flat rooftops, which might be seen as modern equivalents of the pasture.

QUAIL PARTIES: California quail, like many ground-loving birds, are quite reluctant to fly. They prefer to run from danger. After the breeding season has ended, as many as 200 quail may gather to feed on the ground. One or two birds, generally males, always keep a lookout from the vantage point of a nearby tree. Flocks of quail, or any other game birds, are called coveys.

▲ *Mourning doves, with their sad call, are still America's commonest doves, even though they are hunted legally in 31 states. But the extinction earlier this century of the very common passenger pigeon should remind us not to take the mourning dove's survival for granted.*

◄ *Like this California quail, most quail live in the western part of the continent. Each type chooses its own separate habitat, though, and different types of quail are very seldom found together.*

▲ *A chipping sparrow attends to its brood in a nest among pine needles. The nestlings are fed on a protein-rich diet of insects, essential for their development and growth, but will switch to a largely vegetarian diet when they are adults.*

▼ *Common nighthawks have adapted well to suburban life. They are willing to use fence posts for roosting, instead of tree limbs. Like owls, these birds have soft feathers at the edges of their wings, which let them fly silently.*

A male northern flicker ▶ investigates a possible nest hole. If it is suitable, he and his mate will remodel the inside. Together they will hack away at the cavity to produce a layer inside of fresh wood chips, a natural method of keeping the nest clean.

Suburban Dwellers

After a couple of days of ▶ feeding insects to her chicks, this cedar waxwing has switched their diet to that of adults, namely berries.

This brown- ▶ headed cowbird looks innocent, but it can be a menace. For example, it almost wiped out the Kirtland's warbler by laying eggs in the warblers' nests, leaving the warbler nestlings hungry. A cowbird-trapping program has helped end the problem.

A blue jay spreads its wing ▶ so it can preen its feathers properly. Preening is a crucial daily task for a bird. The bird draws its beak along each feather to remove any dirt and parasites. This operation also helps straighten the feathers' barbs, which is vital to keeping flight feathers in precise flying trim. Preening also ensures that the body feathers will insulate the bird properly. Most birds have an oil gland at the base of their tails. Using the beak, the bird spreads the oil on its feathers to keep them flexible, waterproof, and free from fungal and bacterial growths.

Shy singers: The well-tended parks and gardens that people love are also loved by many forest birds. Brown thrashers, for example, have increasingly moved into the suburbs. There, they search for food in their own way—raking through the leaf litter under shrubs and hedges, looking for insects. Wonderful singers, shy brown thrashers have the largest song repertoire of all American birds. An astounding 1,100 song types have been recorded.

Renewing the forest: Blue jays have become a familiar part of suburban life over recent decades. Each fall, they build up an emergency winter food supply by storing beechnuts and acorns in the ground. Many seeds are always left uneaten and sprout to produce new trees. Blue jays, then, help to regenerate forests, which, in turn, helps to renew their own food supplies.

Bird parasites: Brown-headed cowbirds take no part in raising their own young. Instead, they rely on the strong parental instincts of other birds to get their offspring taken care of. The female cowbird lays a single egg in the nest of another bird, which is called the host. Some species, such as blue jays and brown thrashers, are unsuitable as hosts because they eject cowbird eggs from their nests. But song sparrows and many other species will accept a cowbird egg and sit on it along with their own. Because cowbird eggs hatch very quickly, cowbird nestlings get a head start on their nest mates and quickly outgrow them. The little intruders get the lion's share of the food supplies brought by their adopted parents. During a season, a female cowbird may lay 12 eggs, perhaps each in the nest of a different species.

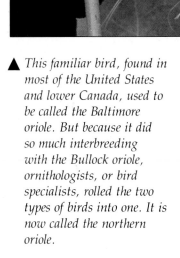

▲ This familiar bird, found in most of the United States and lower Canada, used to be called the Baltimore oriole. But because it did so much interbreeding with the Bullock oriole, ornithologists, or bird specialists, rolled the two types of birds into one. It is now called the northern oriole.

Brown thrashers like to ▶ choose an exposed perch such as this one when they sing. Like their relatives, the northern mockingbirds, thrashers are very good mimics.

Visitors to Bird Feeders

FEEDING YOUR FRIENDS: Wherever you live, you can easily attract birds to your yard or garden by putting out different kinds of food. Winter is the best time, when natural foods are often scarce or trapped under a layer of ice. You can buy or build bird feeders in many different designs, and they are sure to be an endless source of entertainment. Feeding birds in wintertime is a special responsibility, though. Once they begin to depend on you for food, they will look to you for a steady food source until spring. Always place your feeders near shelter, so birds can safely hide from predators like cats or hawks.

Bird feeders are a good way to watch birds from close up and learn more about them. You will soon notice how some birds only feed on the ground, and others happily flock to hanging feeders. Chickadees are especially fun to watch because they are great acrobats. They like to hang upside down to take peanuts from swaying feeders.

SWEETS FOR THE SWEET: You can get special feeders that will dispense a sugary solution to hummingbirds, orioles, and tanagers. When hummingbirds hover to drink from the feeders, their wings beat so fast that they are just a blur. These nectar feeders must be cleaned and filled often or else the sugar will ferment into alcohol, which can be harmful to hummingbirds.

◀ *The unmistakable male northern cardinal actually lives in the eastern and southern United States, where it is loved for its beautiful song as well as its plumage. Its strong beak is designed for crushing seeds.*

WATER FOR LIFE: Birds must bathe regularly year-round to keep their feathers in prime condition. Providing water for drinking and bathing is especially important in dry seasons, when other sources of drinking water are not available.

◀ *This red-bellied woodpecker can be identified as a male by its red crown. It is raiding a bird table filled with seeds. These adaptable birds quickly become very trusting. In some parks, they will even feed from your hand.*

Though they are beating over 50 times each second, the wings of this female ruby-throated hummingbird have been frozen by the photographer's skill. ▶

In woods and gardens ▲ *across North America, the* chick-a-dee-dee-dee *call announces the presence of a passing band of black-capped chickadees.*

Dark-eyed juncos can be ▶ *found all over North America in one season or another. Certain species of juncos have beaks that actually change lengths with the seasons, getting shorter during seed-eating time.*

Barn and Building Nesters

NEW KINDS OF HOMES: As human impact on the environment has increased in the last century, many birds have changed their habits to make use of man-made structures. Pigeons, for instance, once built their flimsy nesting platforms in small caves on sea cliffs. Today they rarely use caves. They choose instead to nest on building ledges or in barns. In fact, pigeons now depend heavily on humans for both food and shelter.

The American kestrel, a small falcon, often lives in and around cities. It hunts house sparrows for the most part and nests in wall cavities or birdhouses. Brought here from Europe, house sparrows are nearly always found near where people live. They raise their young under eaves, on rafters, and in any small opening in a wall or roof.

THE STARLING TAKEOVER: The European starling, another bird brought here from the Old World, has become incredibly successful in its adopted country. Sixty birds were originally set free in New York City a century ago. Now there are an incredible 200 million in the United States—as many starlings as people. City buildings are favorite starling roosting places in winter, and roosting flocks often top one million.

This typical European starling's nest is an untidy jumble of bits and scraps. Tucked under the eaves amid roof insulation, the nest is in a warm, well-protected position.

RATCATCHERS: Common barn owls are easy to spot because they have heart-shaped faces instead of round ones. They do not build real nests but lay their half-dozen or so eggs on bare wood or stone. However, in years when food is plentiful, they lay more eggs, up to 11. In rat plague years, barn owls rear more nestlings and catch far more rats than usual. This makes them valuable friends to farmers.

◀ *Common barn owls are found in most of the United States but are becoming scarce in the East, because development is threatening to wipe out their nesting places.*

City birds are often very ▶ *willing to nest in places that seem very unlikely. This pigeon looks completely at home sitting in a traffic light.*

The house ▶
sparrow, also
called the English
sparrow, is one of the
most common American
birds. One reason it is such a
successful breed is that it is
able to raise as many as three
broods a year.

◀ American kestrels are
able to hover—to rapidly
beat their wings so that
they can stay
motionless in the air.
This lets them scan
the ground for the
smallest
movement of a
tiny mouse or
lizard. During
the summer,
these birds can
live largely on
grasshoppers
or crickets,
often caught
in midair.

BUILT FOR KILLING: Hawks, eagles, falcons, and owls are commonly called raptors, or birds of prey. Because they are meat eaters, they share features such as strongly hooked beaks, sharp talons, and large eyes that give them acute vision. (This is where the common expressions *hawk-eyed* and *eagle-eyed* have come from.) Raptors generally use their strong feet to kill their prey.

DAY AND NIGHT HUNTERS: There are two groups of raptors: daytime and nighttime hunters. The daytime, or diurnal, hunters, like hawks and eagles, use their long claws to hold food while they tear it into pieces with their hooked bills. Nighttime, or nocturnal, raptors, usually do not tear apart their prey. Because the prey is swallowed whole, owls must bring up pellets of material they cannot digest, such as large bones, feathers, and fur.

NO CRASHING: When flying quickly through dense forests, raptors must be able to change direction in an instant to avoid hurting themselves by flying into branches. Northern goshawks are typical forest raptors; they have short wings and long tails, which let them twist and turn at great speeds while chasing down thrushes or gray squirrels. In the underbrush, long wings would do more harm than good.

This young sharp-shinned ▼ *hawk's eyes will be red when it becomes an adult. This raptor preys on birds much more than any other bird of prey does. It lives in most of North America, except for the far South.*

▼ *These are northern saw-whet owls. They get their name from their rasping call, which sounds like a saw being sharpened. These birds live in swamps, bogs, and evergreen forests.*

A great horned owl drops onto its victim, holding out its razor-sharp claws, or talons. Few medium-size mammals or large birds are safe from this efficient hunter, from snowshoe hares and gray squirrels to Canada geese and long-eared owls. Even the skunk's foul smell may not protect it from the great horned owl. Sometimes the owls' nests reek of the powerful odor of skunk.

This northern goshawk ▼ normally preys on hares. The word **raptor** means "one who seizes and carries away."

▼ It is rare for a broad-winged hawk to raise four large chicks like these. The last nestling to hatch is usually much smaller than the others. It often cannot compete for food—and starves.

Ground Dwellers

ADAPTED FOR SURVIVAL: In the forest, many birds seldom take to the trees. They prefer the forest floor as a place to search for food, seek shelter, or build nests. They are so well adapted to forest life that they are quite safe on the ground.

Whippoorwills, for example, sleep during the day, hidden on the forest floor. Their plumage is patterned to camouflage them against a backdrop of leaf mold. They do not build nests but simply lay two eggs on the ground in the sparse undergrowth at the edge of the woods. The whippoorwill's name is inspired by its distinctive call.

INCREDIBLE FLIGHT: During courtship, a male American woodcock tries to impress a possible mate by performing a dramatic display flight at dawn or dusk. He rises up from the ground in a widening spiral, serenading the female with song as he finally flies in a circle 300 feet up in the air. Then he zigzags back to earth like a falling leaf, wings whistling.

STICKING TOGETHER: Bobwhites like to live in groups. Except in nesting season, they congregate on the ground in coveys of about 30 birds. At night, large coveys split into smaller groups of a dozen or so. Each group forms a tightly packed circle, heads facing outward and tails held up. This arrangement allows them to keep watch all around for predators, and it helps to conserve body heat on cold nights.

Rufous-sided towhees make sure they stay in dense thickets as they noisily rake over leaf litter. The foliage protects them from flying predators. Towhees are omnivorous: They eat both plants and animals. Their diet includes insects, spiders, snails, and lizards, as well as seeds and berries.

Male wild turkeys ▶ perform their familiar strutting display early each spring, when their noisy gobblings can be heard over a mile away. Each gobbler's voice deepens as it matures, until it finally reaches a deep, throaty bass.

▼ *Whippoorwills time their nesting season with the moon's cycle. By doing this, parents get the advantage of brightly moonlit nights to hunt for moths to feed their two chicks. This is a vital survival strategy; at other times, their woodland hunting grounds are murky and dark.*

In a sunlit clearing, a ▲ magnificent male ruffed grouse proudly displays his feathers. He may also make a hollow drumming sound by rapidly beating his wings on a log.

This northern ▶ bobwhite, a species of quail, is producing a rising, whistling call. This is meant both to attract a mate and to challenge any nearby rivals. His name, like the whippoorwill's, is inspired by his song.

▲ Ground lovers like this rufous-sided towhee rarely venture out from the undergrowth. As you might guess, the term rufous means reddish.

Birds of the Evergreen Forest

FOLLOWING THE PINE CONES: Birds that feed mostly on conifer seeds, like the seeds of pine cones, sometimes become nomadic; that is, they lead a wandering life instead of staying in one place. Red crossbills, especially, are well known for their periodic migrations, which are called irruptions. These large population movements happen when there are widespread failures in conifer-seed production. Conifer-seed crops go in cycles, and a very good year is often followed by a very poor one. Crossbills raise large broods in good pine years, so their numbers are particularly high in the bad pine years that follow. The birds cannot find enough food and often have to wander far south of their usual range to find better cone harvests.

EVOLUTION'S PRODUCT: Crossbills have been tailor-made by the forces of evolution to make the most of the nutrition in pine cones. Their uniquely crossed bills are perfectly designed for forcing apart the tough scales around pine kernels, so their tongues can free the seeds inside. Individual crossbills are left-handed or right-handed, depending on the side their bills overlap. Pine grosbeaks, on the other hand, have stubby, general-purpose bills for eating a more varied diet.

TREE CLIMBERS: Almost mouselike, brown creepers spiral upward around tree trunks, clinging tightly with long, sharp claws and using their stiff tails to steady themselves. When they reach the top, they fly to the foot of the next tree and start again. They use their down-curved bills to pry out insects and spiders. Creepers skillfully weave nests from shreds of bark, spiderwebs, and mosses, and hide the nests under strips of loose bark.

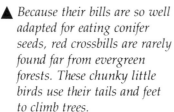

◄ *A creeper searches a lichen-covered tree trunk for food. If disturbed while foraging, these tiny birds press flat against the bark, relying on their camouflage to protect them from predators.*

▼ *Familiar to all who camp in evergreen forests, the gray jay is a particularly bold member of the crow family. Gray jays are unafraid of people. They actively seek humans out, hoping to share their lunches.*

▲ *Because their bills are so well adapted for eating conifer seeds, red crossbills are rarely found far from evergreen forests. These chunky little birds use their tails and feet to climb trees.*

Pine siskins are very ▶ *social and often nest only a few feet apart. Winter flocks can number as many as 1,000 birds. They can be found in most parts of the United States in the cold months.*

▲ *Male pine grosbeaks, like the one above, offer food to their partners as part of their courtship ritual.*

Mixed Woodland Dwellers

TREES OF LIFE: Woodpeckers are woodland birds, and they depend almost totally on trees for their lives. Not only does their food live on or grow on trees, but woodpeckers also chisel out nest holes from tree trunks. They even hammer on dry tree limbs like drums when they want to proclaim their breeding territories, scare off rivals, and attract mates. Acorn woodpeckers use trees for food storage. Families drill holes in tree trunks or branches and then wedge acorns tightly into the storage holes. They fiercely defend their acorn pantries against squirrels, jays, and other woodpeckers. There is a record of one single tree in which a phenomenal 50,000 acorns had been stored.

NO PLACE TO LIVE: The ivory-billed woodpecker is now extinct in the United States. This bird lives in forest swamps with plenty of dead and decaying trees that harbor the bird's main food supply, wood-boring beetle larvae. Logging in this country has destroyed the cypress forests and bottomlands where the ivory-billed woodpecker lived. Several recent expeditions to Cuba were only able to find a couple of individuals. With the world population of these birds so drastically low, it seems inevitable that ivory-billed woodpeckers will disappear forever. If they do, they will be another victim on the list of extinctions brought about by the human race.

◀ *In summer, this male acorn woodpecker drills short holes in oak-tree branches to drink the trees' sugary sap. In spite of their name, acorn woodpeckers feed mostly on insects when they can, only eating acorns when they are in season.*

BRIGHT MALES: Brilliant colors and a sweet song have made rose-breasted grosbeaks popular cage birds in their winter quarters in Mexico. In the wild, the males try to impress potential mates by showing off their rose red breast feathers. Male scarlet tanagers undergo a stunning change each spring, when they replace dull yellow-green feathers with bright scarlet ones. Courting males spread and fold, spread and fold their black wings. This reveals and hides their bright red backs. Male American redstarts get a similar effect by fanning and closing black-and-red tails and wings.

◀ *The scarlet tanager is one of a handful of North American tanagers; most tanagers are tropical. This is among the most brightly colored of all North American birds. It lives in the eastern United States and southern Canada.*

▼ *It is easy to see why this red-eyed vireo has the nickname of little hangnest. The bird's habit of singing all through the heat of a summer's day has earned it another local name, preacher bird. It is also called by a third name, the red-eyed greenlet.*

◀ *Rose-breasted grosbeaks try to raise two broods in a single season whenever they can. In order to better the second family's chances, males tend to the first fledglings while their mates start building the second nest.*

▼ *This female American redstart is perched on the fruit of a pawpaw tree, but it actually rarely eats fruits. It normally eats insects such as wood borers, spittle insects, and leafhoppers.*

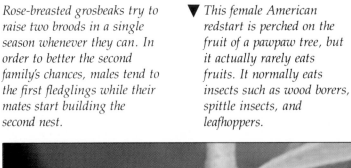

Birds of the Open Woodland

SUGAR LOVERS: Open woodlands have a lot of undergrowth, bushes, and foliage that can grow because more light filters down through the trees than in a dense forest. Yellow-bellied sapsuckers drill through the bark of many trees and shrubs in the open woods, to get at their sugar-rich sap. To lap up the sweet fluid, sapsuckers are equipped with long, brush-tipped tongues. The holes sapsuckers drill are also visited by hummingbirds, warblers, and flying squirrels. They drink the sap or catch insects attracted, and possibly trapped, by the sticky liquid.

As is often the case in the natural world, sapsuckers can both be a nuisance and a help to people. They can cause damage to trees grown for lumber, but they also eat pest insects like tent moth caterpillars. Sapsuckers are part of a complicated ecological balance. This balance is all too easily upset when humans decide to control "pests" like the sapsucker.

SMARTY-BIRDS: Black-billed magpies belong to the crow family. Birds in the crow family are thought to be the most intelligent in the world. They have excellent memories. Unlike most birds, they can count up to three or four, an ability that can cause problems for nature photographers.

Often, when a photographer is trying to shoot a nesting bird, he or she brings along an assistant. The bird flies off a short way. The photographer hides and then the assistant leaves, fooling the bird into thinking that the danger is past, and that it can return to the nest. Crows are not so easily tricked; they can figure out that one human is left. So several assistants must be used to photograph crows successfully.

LONG TAILS: Scissor-tailed flycatchers have tails almost twice as long as their bodies. When males are courting, they perform backward somersaults in the air. This shows off their tails and their pink underwings. They often feed by "flycatching," making short attacks from a perch to snap up insects. Blue-gray gnatcatchers feed in the same way.

▼ *This yellow-bellied sapsucker is sucking some sap from a tree she has just drilled. Sapsuckers are actually types of woodpeckers.*

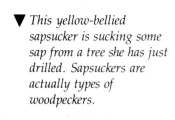

▲ *The scissor-tailed flycatcher is the state bird of Oklahoma. Its long, forked tail makes it easy to see when it perches on power lines or fences.*

▲ The very smart black-billed magpie can be found all over the western part of the United States. Its call sounds like laughing and chuckling.

◄ This blue-gray gnatcatcher's nest cup is quite a feat of architecture. It is woven from plant fibers tightly bound with spider's silk, and lined with bark strips and feathers. Lichens cover its outside.

▲ Yellow-billed cuckoos usually raise their own young, but occasionally they put their eggs in other birds' nests. They often choose black-billed cuckoos to act as foster parents for their young.

Meadows, Prairies, and Scrublands

5

QUICK DEATH: Of all open-country birds of prey, falcons are by far the swiftest, built for speed with long, pointed wings and powerful flight muscles. Keeping low to increase the element of surprise, prairie falcons flush blackbirds or sparrows, then quickly outfly them and seize them in midair with their sharp talons. They will also go after young prairie dogs, pouncing suddenly after a ground-hugging flight.

MEXICAN NEIGHBORS: Even though they don't look much like falcons, crested caracaras belong to the falcon family. They are sometimes called Mexican eagles. These birds are now rare in the United States, because they are losing their desert habitats. The crested caracara is Mexico's national bird, and it is still found in good numbers in Central and South America.

TROUBLE FOR SNAKES: Northern harriers used to be called marsh hawks. They hunt by carefully crisscrossing open marshlands, dropping onto rodents or water snakes unlucky enough to catch their attention. Harriers have ruffs of feathers that channel sound waves to their ears; this gives them somewhat owl-like faces. As you would expect, sound plays an important part in the harrier's hunting.

Black-shouldered kites often hover over an intended victim, getting a fix on it. Then they dive toward the ground to grab their quarry.

▼ *Rough-legged hawks feed on small rodents called lemmings. They may lay twice as many eggs as normal in years when lemming numbers boom. When the lemming population falls drastically, the hawks wander outside their usual nesting range to look for prey.*

A preference for open ▶ farmlands has been a good thing for black-shouldered kites. Unlike most birds of prey, they have increased their numbers as the amount of farmland has increased. By feeding mostly on rodents, always the enemies of farmers, these raptors live in harmony with humans.

Open-Country Hawks and Falcons

▲ In farm regions, prairie falcons absorb pesticide poison when they feed on seed-eating birds. The result is that the eggs the falcons lay have shells that are often too thin to protect the hatchlings, and the offspring die.

▲ You can tell this red-tailed hawk is young because its eyes are yellow. It has such good eyesight, it can spot a field mouse from 100 feet up, about ten stories.

▼ Crested caracaras often spend early mornings scouring roadsides for animals killed by the last night's traffic. They can catch their own prey, but their build is better suited for scavenging. They are not especially fast in the air, so when they do hunt, they often run along the ground. Caracaras were named after their call by the Tupi tribes of South America.

Vultures, Owls, and Nightjars

CLOSE TO THE BRINK: The California condor is one of the world's rarest birds. Unfortunately, it no longer exists in the wild. When there were fewer than 30 of them left, conservationists agonized about what to do. They finally decided to capture all the remaining wild condors in a last-ditch attempt to save them by breeding them in captivity. Since condors do not breed until six years of age and only lay one egg every other year, the chance of success was small. Happily, the program has done better than expected, and the population is slowly building up. But it is hard to foresee condors ever being returned to the wild. Most of their habitat is gone for good.

FLOATING ON AIR: When air is warmed by the sun, it rises in columns known as thermals. Vultures use thermals and mountain updrafts to stay aloft with very little effort for hours on end. Vultures are perfectly designed for soaring flight. Their short, broad wings and spread wing tips allow them to glide at slow speeds without stalling.

Burrowing owls do just that: They live in the ground, in abandoned prairie-dog and ground squirrel burrows. The young of these mammals are often part of the owls' diet. When frightened, young burrowing owls make a distress call strangely like the warning rattle of a prairie rattlesnake, probably to scare away enemies.

SUMMER SLEEPERS: Most people know about animals that hibernate in winter to escape the cold and food shortages. But it is not so well known that desert animals do it, too, to avoid

prey shortages brought on by heat and lack of water in summer. This summer hibernation is called estivation. Lesser nighthawks and common poorwills, both members of the nightjar family, are the only birds in the world that have been discovered estivating. One poorwill was found dormant under a desert rock for three years running. No wonder the poorwill is known to the Hopi, Native Americans of Arizona, as *Holchko*—"the sleeping one."

Photographed at night, ▶ *the eye of this poorwill appears red. This is caused by a reflection of the camera flash's light from the eye into the camera lens.*

Much of a black vulture's diet is accidentally provided by man. Road kills, garbage dumps, fish wharves, and slaughterhouses all provide food for these very useful birds. By clearing away rotting carcasses, they act as a natural control against the spread of disease.

◀ *The California condor, with its enormous nine-foot wingspan, must have been quite a sight in the wild. It has been brought to the edge of extinction because human development has left it nowhere to live.*

▼ *Its long legs are a good clue that this burrowing owl is a ground dweller. They are good diggers but usually only enlarge deserted rodent tunnels. Sadly, antirodent campaigns also threaten these owls.*

A turkey vulture basks ▶ in the sun. As a scavenger, it has much weaker feet than the strong talons of other raptors. With its acute sense of smell, the turkey vulture is better at finding food than its more common relative, the black vulture; often it must share its food with black vultures.

Birds of Fields and Meadows

SUCCESS STORY: The amazing increase in the range of cattle egrets over the last century is a modern-day wildlife success story. With almost no help from humans, these small herons have spread from their African homeland into Europe, Asia, and the Americas. They have even gone to the Galápagos Islands, 600 miles off the coast of Ecuador in South America. The expanding and shrinking of animal ranges is a natural process and should only cause concern when human activities speed it up unnaturally.

SUMMER VISITORS: Barn swallows are another great success story, one of the few helped along by humans. Since people started putting up more and more buildings, providing places for the birds to nest, the barn swallow population has grown tremendously. Barn swallows visit North America only in summer, migrating to South America every winter. To North Americans, swallows are a sure sign of spring. They are fine fliers and get all their food by snatching insects in midair.

The eastern kingbird, another summer visitor, is part of a group of birds called tyrant flycatchers. In fact, it is from the kingbird that the whole group gets its name. It is so fearless that Native Americans called it "little chief."

JUST PRETENDING: Killdeers are widespread meadow birds. They will draw predators away from eggs or chicks by pretending to have a broken wing. This artful performance involves calling and dragging a partly open wing along the ground. It is so convincing that a predator is lured after the adult bird, which then surprises its foe by flying off when its young are safe.

American goldfinches are irresistibly attracted to thistle, dandelion, and sunflower seed heads.

▲ Eastern kingbirds will not hesitate to attack much larger birds to defend their nests. Hawks and crows are often chased out of kingbird territory.

Cattle egrets feed on insects that swarm around cows. They also perch on top of these animals to pick off ticks; their popular name in Africa is the tickbird. ▶

They use them for food and also line their nests with thistledown. Barn swallows, on the other hand, collect feathers or horsehair to cushion their eggs. They build nests from pellets of mud laced with straw and dried by the sun, much in the way adobe houses are made.

Perched on a new spring ▶ *shoot, a glorious male American goldfinch pauses between bursts of song. Occasionally, these birds will become so entangled in burdock burrs, while eating the plant's seeds, that they cannot escape.*

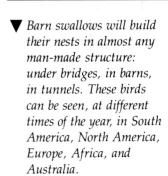

This killdeer and its chicks ▶ *have distinct black and white bands. These break up the birds' outlines so they blend in with the mottled background, making them almost invisible.*

▼ *Barn swallows will build their nests in almost any man-made structure: under bridges, in barns, in tunnels. These birds can be seen, at different times of the year, in South America, North America, Europe, Africa, and Australia.*

Prairie Residents

COMPETITION FOR FOOD: Many of America's endless prairie grasslands have now been replaced by huge farms that may grow miles and miles of a single grain. These farms represent a sea of food to grain-eating birds like bobolinks. But when large migrating flocks of these birds descend on the fields of grain, they must come into conflict with farmers. Around the turn of the century, bobolinks by the millions devastated rice fields in the south. As a result, they were hunted so thoroughly that the bobolink population, reduced drastically, has not recovered since.

THE PRAIRIE CHICKEN DANCE: Greater prairie chickens have unusual breeding habits. Before the breeding season, the males take up their places at a lek. This is a traditional location used by rival males to display to potential mates. Each male defends his own small area in the lekking ground, where he performs a ritual dance for any females who come near. The males inflate their orange neck sacs, put up neck crests, raise their tails, half open their wings, and make a deep, booming sound. After choosing the most impressive male, a female leaves the lek right after mating. She will build a nest and raise her young without help from her partner.

◀ *In their breeding plumage, male bobolinks are black and white, with tan necks. In fall, they look very much like females or young birds, which makes it difficult for bird-watchers to tell them apart. Like many grassland birds, bobolinks are ground nesters, coarsely braiding the stems of grasses into a shallow cup hidden in a meadow. Though males do not help sit on the eggs, they do bring food to the nestlings.*

The mowing of fields and meadows during breeding season is a grave hazard for ground-nesting birds such as eastern meadowlarks. Adult birds can escape by slipping away from the nest, but their eggs and nestlings are often crushed by the farm machinery. Luckily, meadowlarks try to raise two broods in a single year, so they often have a chance to make up for their losses.

▲ *Western meadowlarks, like this one in full song, usually prefer drier habitats than the eastern species. They also tend to be somewhat less brightly colored. But where their ranges overlap, western and eastern meadowlarks often interbreed.*

◀ *Over most of America, loggerhead shrikes are declining in numbers. The reasons for this are not absolutely clear, but the loss of habitat is certainly one cause. Also, because the birds eat mainly insects, pesticide poisoning is another likely reason for their decline.*

STORING FOOD: Just as jays store acorns, loggerhead shrikes make "pantries" of crickets, frogs, and even small birds, skewering them on thorns or barbed wire. The corpses are usually eaten within a few days or a week. Shrikes only store what they can eat, unlike jays and acorn woodpeckers, which create enormous stockpiles.

Prairie habitats have one chief ▶ problem for birds: a lack of natural lookout points from which they can watch out for rivals and predators. A fence post is supplying this upland sandpiper with a handy solution. It has an excellent view of its territory.

Desert Inhabitants

HELP FROM CACTI: Deserts make tough demands on plants and animals. They have to withstand the extremes of daytime heat, nighttime cold, and year-round dryness. Cacti are well-adapted desert plants, and their success is vital to the survival of many desert birds.

HOMES TO SHARE: Gila woodpeckers chisel nesting cavities in saguaro or giant cactus trunks but do not use them right away. They wait until the cactus sap has had enough time to harden. Saguaro nest holes offer good insulation from both heat and cold—so good, in fact, that many other birds try to take over Gila woodpecker nests.

Elf owls depend entirely upon woodpeckers for nesting places. They often must defend their secondhand homes from other small birds. In deserts, elf owls use nesting holes made by Gila woodpeckers, but in more wooded habitats, they use homes provided by acorn, golden-fronted, or Strickland's woodpeckers.

Cactus wrens build bulb-shaped nests with a short passageway that leads to a shaded central chamber. Made of grasses and plant fibers, the nests are built atop cholla cacti or tree yuccas. Each pair of cactus wrens builds several nests. Cacti also produce fruits that cactus wrens like.

BEEP, BEEP! Roadrunners have long, muscular legs that are well suited for high-speed dashes after crickets and lizards. It has been hard for scientists to sift facts out from folklore about these birds, but experts do claim to have clocked roadrunners at speeds of 15 to 20 miles per hour!

◀ *In some areas, Harris's hawks hunt in groups. Their teamwork is probably not planned, but it does work. When one bird flies to the ground to chase a rabbit, it catches the attention of nearby hawks. If the rabbit runs in their direction, they will head it off. Unless the rabbit can quickly find a safe hiding place, it is soon caught, and its carcass is shared by all.*

Peering out of its ▶ saguaro nest hole, an elf owl prepares to set off on the night's hunt. It will search for moths, crickets, even scorpions. The scorpions are only eaten after their stings have been removed.

▼ Gila woodpeckers live in cactus country, but they can sometimes be enticed to backyard bird feeders. They like standard bird foods such as suet, but they especially like watermelon, which may remind them of water-filled cactus.

▲ A cactus wren keeps a lookout from its prickly perch. When foraging, it uses its bill to pry up leaves to dislodge any insects, spiders, or lizards underneath. Cactus wrens eat more plant matter than do other wrens—up to 20 percent of their diet.

▼ Surprisingly, roadrunners are actually a type of ground cuckoo. Displaying males strut with heads high and wings and tails drooped low. The roadrunner's song, delivered from a perch on a cactus, is a hoarse coo-coo-coo-ooh-ooh-ooh.

53

Mountains and Arctic Tundra

6

AS RUGGED AS THE TUNDRA: The tundra, the half-frozen, treeless country of the Arctic, is a demanding environment. Few birds can withstand these Alaskan and Canadian plains year-round. Only two raptors, the gyrfalcon and the snowy owl, are hardy enough to survive the tundra.

The white phase gyrfalcon (pronounced JER-falcon) is surely one of the most impressive of all raptors. As with many birds of prey, female gyrfalcons are larger than their mates. The reason for this is not clear. One possibility is that the size difference allows each sex to feed on different prey species. This would eliminate competition for food between mates.

LOOKING FOR LEMMINGS: Snowy owls, like rough-legged hawks, finely tune their breeding cycles to changes in the lemming population. In good lemming years, snowy owls will lay as many as 13 eggs. When lemming numbers go down, the owls lay fewer eggs. And when the lemming population crashes, snowy owls may have to abandon the tundra and can wander as far south as Alabama.

Before a 1962 law ▶
protected golden eagles,
20,000 of them
were wrongly shot as
lamb killers.

ONE BIRD, ONE NAME: The small gray-brown owl known in America as the boreal owl is called a Tengmalm's owl in England, and a rough-legged screech owl in Germany. This could be a very confusing situation for scientists and bird-watchers. But thanks to a Swedish scientist named Carolus Linnaeus, it is not. In 1758, he created an international system for naming every living species of plant or animal. Each species is given a two-part Latin name. The first word is the genus, a name for a group of related species. The second word is the name given only to that species. So, boreal owls are known as *Aegolius funereus* all over the world.

▲ Peregrine falcons look after the offspring in their nest very carefully, delicately offering the nestlings strips of meat until the chicks can tear up their own food.

▼ Because there are no trees on the tundra, snowy owls perch on rocks, grassy hummocks, telephone poles, or rooftops.

▲ This magnificent great gray owl is America's largest owl. It is not the heaviest, however, because it is not as stoutly built as a horned or snowy owl. Like many animals that live in the northern forests, great gray owls allow people to get very close to them.

▲ A gyrfalcon, camouflaged against its rocky background, watches for movement of its prey. This bird has the falcon's typical long, pointed wings, rather short tail, and streamlined body.

Water Birds of the North

PRECIOUS TIME: For a brief period every summer, the frozen Arctic plains melt a little. A vast network of shallow pools, teeming with life, appears. Before the last snows have vanished, migrant water birds begin arriving to stake their claims to nesting territories, often the very same ones used in previous years. Because time is so short, many water birds choose their mates before flying north, and partnerships often last for life. These ways of behaving are vital time-savers that make the most of the time available for rearing young before winter blizzards return.

DOWN FOR WARMTH: Arctic temperatures can plummet below zero even in summer. Since eggs are extremely vulnerable to cold, they must be kept warm at all times. No eggs are better safeguarded than those of eiders. Like many other ducks, eiders pluck down from their own breasts to line their nests and cover their eggs whenever they must leave them to feed. Nothing insulates as well as eiderdown, which is why it is popular with humans for use in sleeping bags and comforters. When they are only two days old, eider ducklings leave the nest with their mothers and move to other feeding grounds. Eiders often give up the care of their ducklings to other adult females, which look after large "nurseries."

THE ENDS OF THE EARTH: Arctic terns are the greatest travelers of all. They are famed for incredible yearly migrations that cover 22,000 miles, from the Arctic Circle to the Antarctic and back. Arctic terns spend more of their lifetimes in sunlight than do any other animal. This is because daylight lasts for nearly 24 hours in polar regions during the summer months—and Arctic terns are present for both northern and southern summers.

▲ *Long-tailed jaegers perform beautiful acrobatics in the air when they are courting. Like their larger relatives, the great skuas, long-tailed jaegers will repeatedly attack any animals that approach their nests, knowingly or unwittingly. They will even attack humans. All trespassers are dived at and may be struck until they move away.*

▲ Hunched low on her nest, this female common eider may not feed at all during the month required to incubate her eggs. She may leave her nest briefly to drink.

◄ As female snow geese mature, they "practice" each year until they learn to lay eggs earlier in the season. This allows their goslings to have longer to learn to fly before the Arctic snows return.

▼ An Arctic tern pauses on a rock before taking a sand eel to its waiting chick. Fish like these form most of their diet, but these birds will eat shellfish now and then. Arctic tern chicks leave their nest within two or three days of hatching and take shelter in nearby vegetation.

◄ This flock of tundra swans will soon leave their icebound winter quarters. These heavy birds save energy on their migrations by flying in a V-shaped formation. It is thought that all except the lead bird get extra lift from air currents caused by the bird in front. The birds regularly change places, so the task of leading the group is shared. Formation flying also helps swans avoid collisions in fog.

Wading Birds and Game Birds

GAME BIRDS: The term *game birds* used to refer only to a group of related bird families that included grouse, turkeys, quails, and prairie chickens. More and more, though, the term has come to mean any bird that can be legally hunted. Certain ducks, geese, doves, and woodcocks are now often called game birds.

BIRD SNOWSHOES: The ptarmigan, a type of grouse, has heavily feathered feet that act like snowshoes to prevent the bird from sinking into soft snow. Quite hardy, rock ptarmigan are among the select few birds that do not migrate south during the Arctic winter. Instead, they molt into snow-white plumage and get their food from whatever tree buds, seeds, and bark can be found above, or dug up from under, the snow line. Their winter coloration is a good camouflage against snowy backdrops and is a vital defense against attack by gyrfalcons.

THE DANCE OF LIFE: Sandhill cranes are tall wading birds, best known for their elaborate dancing rituals. These dances cement bonds between pairs of these faithful birds, which

When it is ▶ not nesting season, whimbrels live on tidal flats. They probe the mud exposed at low tide for fiddler crabs.

Chukar come from Asia but ▶ have been brought to many parts of America. These birds, a kind of partridge, have become so well established in some areas that it is now legal to hunt them.

usually form lifetime partnerships. At times, their gray color becomes stained reddish brown. This is a result of digging in soil rich in iron oxide, or rust.

Though closely related and similar-looking, whimbrels and long-billed curlews like very different habitats in breeding season. Whimbrels nest on open tundra, while the curlews settle on high ground, or uplands. Both species, however, can be found on coastal mud flats during the winter.

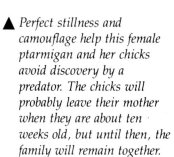

▲ Perfect stillness and camouflage help this female ptarmigan and her chicks avoid discovery by a predator. The chicks will probably leave their mother when they are about ten weeks old, but until then, the family will remain together.

▼ Unusual in the bird world, this female red-necked phalarope is much prettier than her mate. He sits on the eggs, because her brighter colors would make her more of a target for predators. Male phalaropes also do all the caring for their chicks during the three weeks before they fly from the nest.

▲ Some breeds of sandhill cranes are migratory, like the ones pictured here near a flock of snow geese. Others remain in one spot. Even though migrating can be dangerous, the sandhill cranes that migrate have survived better than their stay-at-home relatives. There are three types that stay in one place; all have small populations, and two are facing possible extinction.

Mountain Songbirds

SINGERS: Nearly two-thirds of the world's bird species are songbirds. They are also called passerines, from the Latin name for the house sparrow. It is impossible to name here all the songbirds, but they include crows, finches, swallows, and wrens. Every songbird has one backward- and three forward-facing toes. This special feature enables songbirds to grip perches tightly, which explains yet another collective name, perching birds.

Clark's nutcrackers have very good memories, which help them survive. They can relocate pinion nuts (the seeds of the pinion pine) hidden months earlier, by memorizing nearby landmarks. Since they may hide many thousands of seeds in a season, this is quite a feat.

Pinion jays, members of the crow family, also adore pinion seeds. They like to live in colonies, with up to 150 nests scattered over a fairly large area. They flock together when feeding and always post a few sentries to warn of approaching hawks.

◀ Common ravens are quick learners, so they become very shy of people where they are hunted. On the other hand, in some places, people appreciate them for helping clean up dead animal carcasses. Where people like them, ravens can become quite tame.

Steller's jays ▶ steal songbird eggs, as this one is doing. This is not as terrible as people think, however. All birds risk attack by predators, and they deal with this threat by laying more eggs or caring longer for their young. Jays are no more of a threat to songbirds than other predators are.

Evening grosbeaks used to live only in the western part of the continent. But they have been moving steadily eastward since the turn of the century. They have probably been following the more widespread planting of their favorite species of food trees. Also, backyard bird feeders generously filled with sunflower seeds have helped them survive.

Mountain chickadees live as high up as 10,000 feet in the nesting season, almost two miles in the air. They move to lower altitudes once their young have flown.

In wintertime, Clark's nutcrackers are known to dig through a thick layer of snow to retrieve pine cones they buried in the fall.

Many woodland songbirds form mixed feeding parties with members of several other species, especially during the winter months. Mountain chickadees, brown creepers, sparrows, and warblers may group together while looking for food. This behavior may increase all the birds' chances of finding plentiful food sources.

Evening grosbeaks sometimes eat road salt, in an attempt to get enough of certain chemicals that they need for proper nutrition. This can be dangerous; it has led to highway accidents in winter when the birds gather on roads to eat the salt put out to melt the snow.

Songbirds of the North

GROUNDED: Because there are no trees on the frozen plains of the north, most of the songbirds that live there make their nests on the ground or in bushes. Water pipits, for example, like to make their nests in clumps of grass. Most male songbirds advertise for a mate by singing from a high perch, but since water pipits cannot do this, they deliver their courtship songs in flight. Pale pipits fly straight up in the air for about 150 feet, about 15 stories up, all the while singing a quiet, tinkling song.

Like many Arctic birds, rosy finches are not afraid of people and will often let them come very close. Rosy finches all have an unusual feature: a pouch inside their mouths, which they use to carry food to their young.

BRRRRR: American tree sparrows usually live around the edges of the tundra and do not go too far into it. Lapland longspurs are found nearer to the North Pole, circling the globe in North America, Europe, and Asia. Snow buntings and common redpolls are also found throughout the far north. Snow buntings are so at home in snow that they even take baths in it. They can survive temperatures down to 50 degrees below zero by burrowing under snow, which is actually a good insulator and helps to keep the buntings warm. Even so, snow buntings are affected by the unpredictable weather in the far north. Sometimes large numbers of them die when late-spring snowstorms blanket their food supplies. In spite of this danger, snow buntings venture farther north than any other land bird does.

◄ *When nesting, a female water pipit does something that some other birds also do: She develops a feather-free patch of skin on her belly. This is called an incubation patch. It lets heat pass more easily from the sitting bird to her eggs, which keeps them warmer.*

◀ Common redpolls have an unusual feature that helps them withstand brutal winters. A pocket partway down a redpoll's throat stores seeds to be eaten later. This allows redpolls to collect large amounts of food at one time. That way, they can spend less time in freezing conditions that could kill them.

Birds normally change ▶ their colors by molting, or changing feathers. Not snow buntings, though. They lose their winter plumage by rubbing away certain feathers, revealing more brightly colored ones underneath. This process is most dramatic in male snow buntings, which get a striking black-and-white pattern each spring.

◀ This female Lapland longspur sits in her nest, tucked away in the tundra's low vegetation. Because Arctic breeding seasons are so short, only a few days can be spent building the nest. When a brood of young longspurs fledges, or grows its flight feathers, it splits into two groups. The parents each feed and protect one group, until the young ones can fend for themselves.

▼ American tree sparrows breed all along the tundra's southern edge. There they find stunted trees and tufts of grass, under which they can hide nests woven from grasses, bark, and moss. They use feathers or fur to make soft beds on which to lay their eggs. Only three weeks after incubation starts, the nestlings are ready to leave.

Further Reading about Birds

Coomber, Richard. *A Photographic Encyclopedia of Birds*. New York: Gallery Books, 1990.

Dobkin, David S., Paul R. Ehrlich, and Darryl Wheye. *The Birder's Handbook*. New York: Simon & Schuster, Inc., 1988.

Forshaw, Joseph, ed. *Encyclopedia of Birds*. New York: Smithmark Publishers Inc., 1991.

Peterson, Roger Tory. *Peterson's Field Guides to the Birds*. Boston: Houghton Mifflin Company, 1980.

Shaw, Frank. *Birds of America*. New York: Gallery Books, 1990.

Picture Credits

Index